TENOR SAX

101 CHRISTMAS SONGS

T0039487

Note: The keys in this book do not match the other wind instruments.

Available for
FLUTE, CLARINET, ALTO SAX, TENOR SAX, TRUMPET,
HORN, TROMBONE, VIOLIN, VIOLA, CELLO

ISBN 978-1-5400-3023-8

Visit Hal Leonard Online at
www.halleonard.com

Contact Us:
Hal Leonard
7777 West Bluemound Road
Milwaukee, WI 53213
Email: info@halleonard.com

In Europe contact:
Hal Leonard Europe Limited
42 Wigmore Street
Marylebone, London, W1U 2RN
Email: info@halleonardeurope.com

In Australia contact:
Hal Leonard Australia Pty. Ltd.
4 Lentara Court
Cheltenham, Victoria, 3192 Australia
Email: info@halleonard.com.au

CONTENTS

ALL I WANT FOR CHRISTMAS IS YOU

TENOR SAX

Words and Music by MARIAH CAREY
and WALTER AFANASIEFF

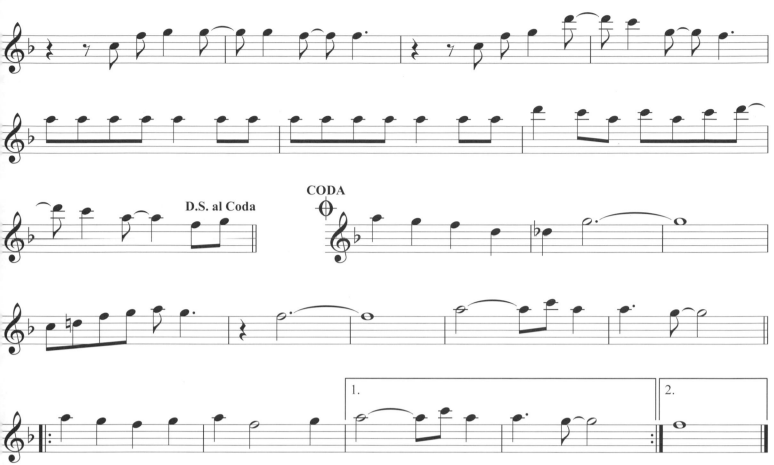

ANGELS FROM THE REALMS OF GLORY

Words by JAMES MONTGOMERY
Music by HENRY T. SMART

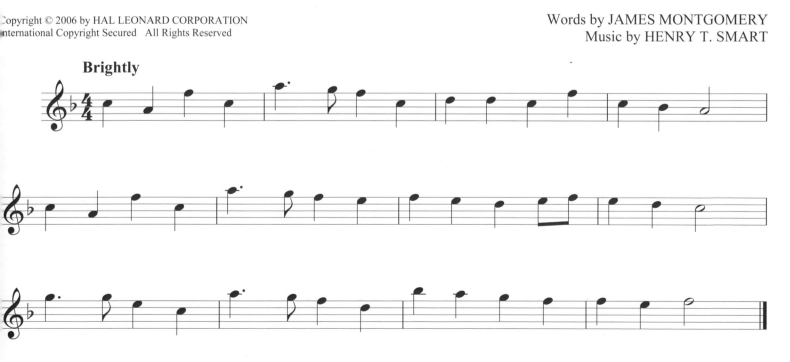

AS LONG AS THERE'S CHRISTMAS

from BEAUTY AND THE BEAST - THE ENCHANTED CHRISTMAS

TENOR SAX

Music by RACHEL PORTMAN
Lyrics by DON BLACK

AULD LANG SYNE

TENOR SAX

Words by ROBERT BURNS
Traditional Scottish Melody

ANGELS WE HAVE HEARD ON HIGH

Traditional French Carol

AWAY IN A MANGER

Music by JAMES R. MURRAY

Slowly

BABY, IT'S COLD OUTSIDE

TENOR SAX

By FRANK LOESSER

Moderately

AWAY IN A MANGER

TENOR SAX

Music by JONATHAN E. SPILMAN

BECAUSE IT'S CHRISTMAS
(For All the Children)

Music by BARRY MANILOW
Lyric by BRUCE SUSSMAN and JACK FELDMAN

BELIEVE

from Warner Bros. Pictures' THE POLAR EXPRESS

TENOR SAX

Words and Music by GLEN BALLARD
and ALAN SILVESTRI

Moderately slow

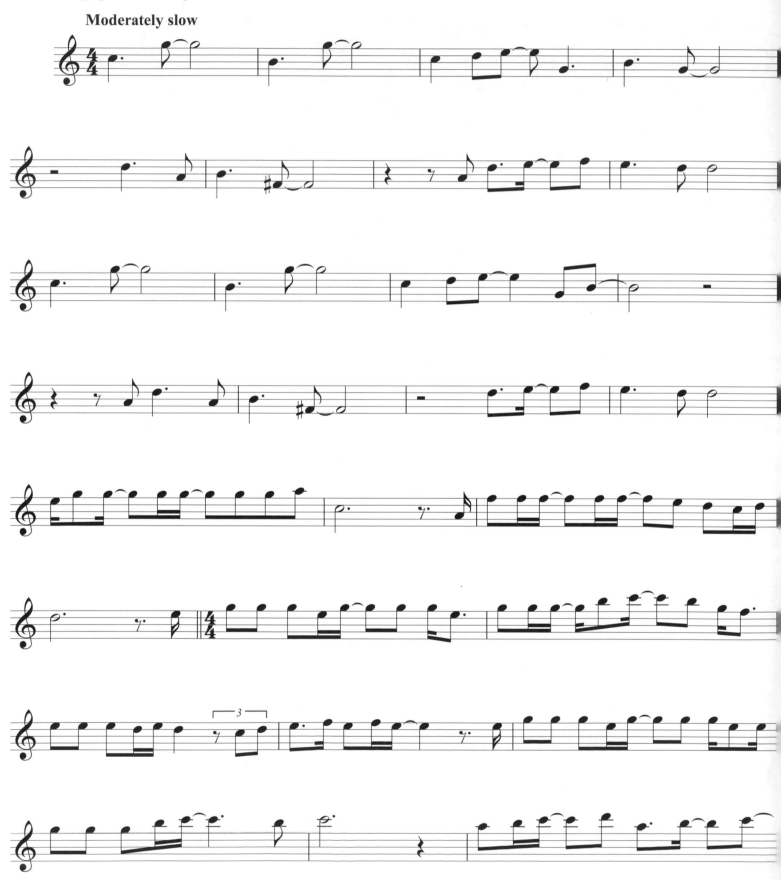

BLUE CHRISTMAS

Words and Music by BILLY HAYES
and JAY JOHNSON

BRAZILIAN SLEIGH BELLS

TENOR SAX

By PERCY FAITH

Bright Samba

To Coda

TENOR SAX

CAROLING, CAROLING

Words by WIHLA HUTSON
Music by ALFRED BURT

THE BELLS OF ST. MARY'S

TENOR SAX

Traditional
Words by DOUGLAS FURBER
Music by A. EMMETT ADAMS

A CHILD IS BORN

TENOR SAX

By THAD JONES

Slowly

THE CHIPMUNK SONG

Words and Music by
ROSS BAGDASARIAN

Happily

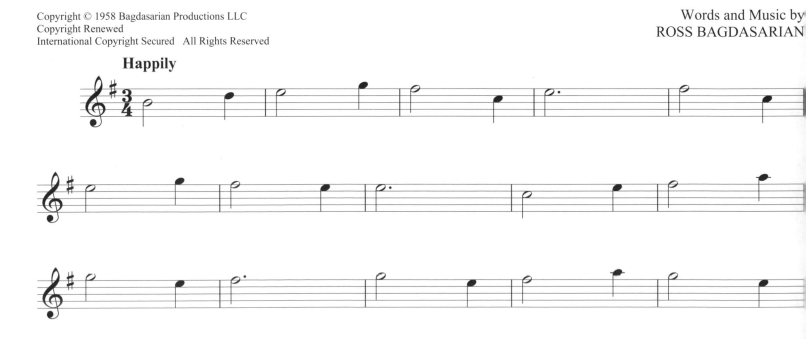

CHRISTMAS IN KILLARNEY

Words and Music by JOHN REDMOND
and FRANK WELDON

Moderately, with a lilt

CHRISTMAS
(Baby Please Come Home)

TENOR SAX

Words and Music by PHIL SPECTOR,
ELLIE GREENWICH and JEFF BARRY

CHRISTMAS IS A-COMIN'
(May God Bless You)

TENOR SAX

Words and Music by
FRANK LUTHER

THE CHRISTMAS SONG
(Chestnuts Roasting on an Open Fire)

TENOR SAX

Music and Lyric by MEL TORMÉ
and ROBERT WELLS

Moderately

DO YOU WANT TO BUILD A SNOWMAN?

from FROZEN

TENOR SAX

Music and Lyrics by KRISTEN ANDERSON-LOPEZ
and ROBERT LOPEZ

COLD DECEMBER NIGHT

TENOR SAX

Words and Music by MICHAEL BUBLE,
ALAN CHANG and ROBERT ROCK

CHRISTMAS TIME IS HERE
from A CHARLIE BROWN CHRISTMAS

TENOR SAX

Words by LEE MENDELSON
Music by VINCE GUARALDI

Slowly

THE CHRISTMAS WALTZ

Words by SAMMY CAHN
Music by JULE STYNE

Moderately, with expression

DANCE OF THE SUGAR PLUM FAIRY
from THE NUTCRACKER

By PYOTR IL'YICH TCHAIKOVSKY

DECK THE HALL

TENOR SAX

Traditional Welsh Carol

DO YOU HEAR WHAT I HEAR

Words and Music by NOEL REGNEY
and GLORIA SHAYNE

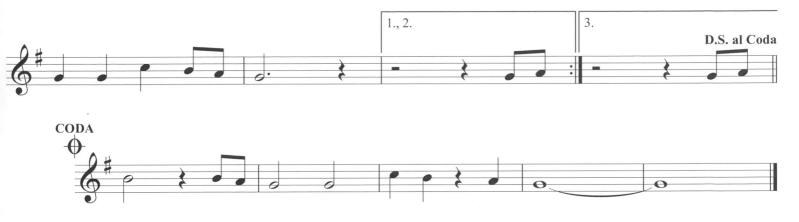

THE FIRST NOEL

17th Century English Carol
Music from W. Sandys' *Christmas Carols*

FAIRYTALE OF NEW YORK

TENOR SAX

Words and Music by JEREMY FINER
and SHANE MacGOWAN

GOD REST YE MERRY, GENTLEMEN

Traditional English Carol

FELIZ NAVIDAD

TENOR SAX

Music and Lyrics by
JOSÉ FELICIANO

GRANDMA GOT RUN OVER BY A REINDEER

TENOR SAX

Words and Music by
RANDY BROOKS

THE GREATEST GIFT OF ALL

TENOR SAX

Words and Music by
JOHN JARVIS

Moderately slow

GOOD KING WENCESLAS

Words by JOHN M. NEALE
Music from *Piae Cantiones*

Moderately

GROWN-UP CHRISTMAS LIST

TENOR SAX

Words and Music by DAVID FOSTER
and LINDA THOMPSON-JENNER

Moderately slow

HARK! THE HERALD ANGELS SING

Words by CHARLES WESLEY
Music by FELIX MENDELSSOHN-BARTHOLDY

HAPPY XMAS
(War Is Over)

TENOR SAX

Written by JOHN LENNON
and YOKO ONO

HAVE YOURSELF A MERRY LITTLE CHRISTMAS

from MEET ME IN ST. LOUIS

TENOR SAX

Words and Music by HUGH MARTIN
and RALPH BLANE

Moderately slow

HAPPY HOLIDAY
from the Motion Picture Irving Berlin's HOLIDAY INN

TENOR SAX

Words and Music by
IRVING BERLIN

Slowly

HARD CANDY CHRISTMAS
from THE BEST LITTLE WHOREHOUSE IN TEXAS

Words and Music by
CAROL HALL

Moderately

HERE COMES SANTA CLAUS
(Right Down Santa Claus Lane)

Words and Music by GENE AUTRY
and OAKLEY HALDEMAN

TENOR SAX

(There's No Place Like)
HOME FOR THE HOLIDAYS

Words and Music by AL STILLMAN
and ROBERT ALLEN

Moderately

I HEARD THE BELLS ON CHRISTMAS DAY

TENOR SAX

Words by HENRY WADSWORTH LONGFELLOW
Music by JOHN BAPTISTE CALKIN

Moderately slow

A HOLLY JOLLY CHRISTMAS

Music and Lyrics by
JOHNNY MARKS

Moderately bright

I WANT A HIPPOPOTAMUS FOR CHRISTMAS
(Hippo the Hero)

TENOR SAX

Words and Music by
JOHN ROX

I'LL BE HOME FOR CHRISTMAS

Words and Music by KIM GANNON
and WALTER KENT

Slowly

I HEARD THE BELLS ON CHRISTMAS DAY

TENOR SAX

Words by HENRY WADSWORTH LONGFELLOW
Adapted by JOHNNY MARKS
Music by JOHNNY MARKS

I SAW MOMMY KISSING SANTA CLAUS

Words and Music by
TOMMIE CONNOR

I SAW THREE SHIPS

TENOR SAX

Traditional English Carol

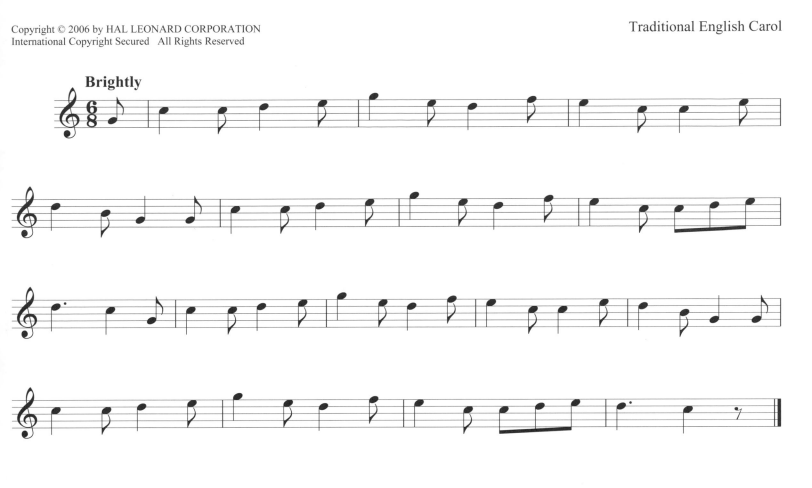

I WONDER AS I WANDER

By JOHN JACOB NILES

I'VE GOT MY LOVE TO KEEP ME WARM

from the 20th Century Fox Motion Picture ON THE AVENUE

TENOR SAX

Words and Music by
IRVING BERLIN

Bright Jump tempo

IT'S BEGINNING TO LOOK LIKE CHRISTMAS

TENOR SAX

By MEREDITH WILLSON

IT MUST HAVE BEEN THE MISTLETOE

(Our First Christmas)

TENOR SAX

By JUSTIN WILDE
and DOUG KONECKY

IT CAME UPON THE MIDNIGHT CLEAR

Words by EDMUND H. SEARS
Traditional English Melody
Adapted by ARTHUR SULLIVAN

Moderately

JINGLE BELLS

TENOR SAX

Words and Music by
J. PIERPONT

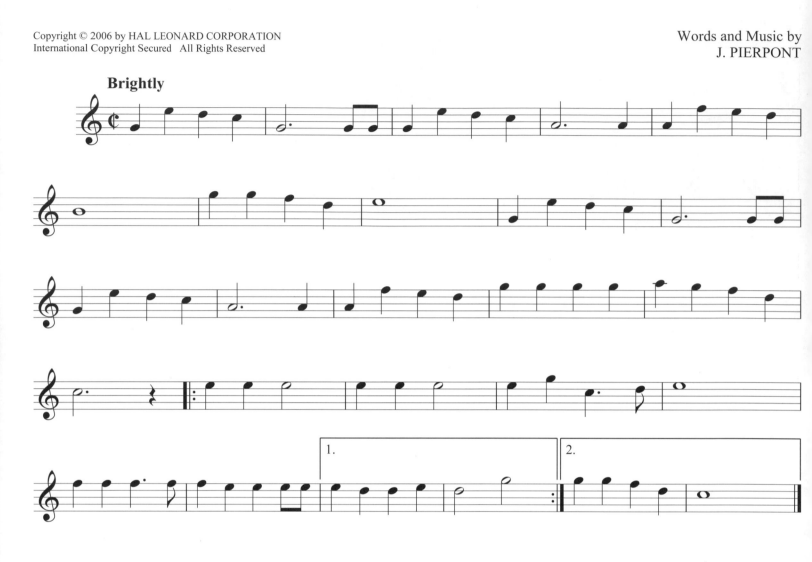

THE LAST MONTH OF THE YEAR
(What Month Was Jesus Born In?)

Words and Music by VERA HALL
Adapted and Arranged by RUBY PICKENS TARTT
and ALAN LOMAX

LET IT SNOW! LET IT SNOW! LET IT SNOW!

Words by SAMMY CAHN
Music by JULE STYNE

JOY TO THE WORLD

TENOR SAX

Words by ISAAC WATTS
Music by GEORGE FRIDERIC HANDEL

Brightly

MARY'S LITTLE BOY CHILD

Words and Music by
JESTER HAIRSTON

Slowly and simply

LITTLE SAINT NICK

TENOR SAX

Words and Music by BRIAN WILSON
and MIKE LOVE

MARCH OF THE TOYS

from BABES IN TOYLAND

TENOR SAX

By VICTOR HERBERT

With spirit

(small note optional)

A MARSHMALLOW WORLD

TENOR SAX

Words by CARL SIGMAN
Music by PETER DE ROSE

MARY, DID YOU KNOW?

TENOR SAX

Words and Music by MARK LOWRY
and BUDDY GREENE

MERRY CHRISTMAS, DARLING

TENOR SAX

Words and Music by RICHARD CARPENTER
and FRANK POOLER

THE MOST WONDERFUL TIME OF THE YEAR

TENOR SAX

Words and Music by EDDIE POLA
and GEORGE WYLE

Brightly, in one

MY FAVORITE THINGS
from THE SOUND OF MUSIC

TENOR SAX

Lyrics by OSCAR HAMMERSTEIN II
Music by RICHARD RODGERS

Lively

MELE KALIKIMAKA

TENOR SAX

Words and Music by
R. ALEX ANDERSON

Brightly

MISTER SANTA

Words and Music by
PAT BALLARD

Bright

MISTLETOE AND HOLLY

Words and Music by FRANK SINATRA,
DOK STANFORD and HENRY W. SANICOLA

Medium Bounce

O LITTLE TOWN OF BETHLEHEM

TENOR SAX

Words by PHILLIPS BROOKS
Music by LEWIS H. REDNER

O HOLY NIGHT

French words by PLACIDE CAPPEAU
English words by JOHN S. DWIGHT
Music by ADOLPHE ADAM

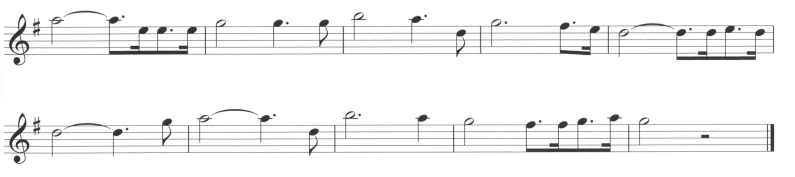

SANTA CLAUS IS COMIN' TO TOWN

Words by HAVEN GILLESPIE
Music by J. FRED COOTS

O CHRISTMAS TREE

TENOR SAX

Traditional German Carol

O COME, ALL YE FAITHFUL

Music by JOHN FRANCIS WADE

PARADE OF THE WOODEN SOLDIERS

TENOR SAX

English Lyrics by BALLARD MacDONALD
Music by LEON JESSEL

PRETTY PAPER

TENOR SAX

Words and Music by
WILLIE NELSON

ROCKIN' AROUND THE CHRISTMAS TREE

TENOR SAX

Music and Lyrics by
JOHNNY MARKS

RUDOLPH THE RED-NOSED REINDEER

TENOR SAX

Music and Lyrics by
JOHNNY MARKS

SANTA BABY

TENOR SAX

By JOAN JAVITS,
PHIL SPRINGER and TONY SPRINGER

SHAKE ME I RATTLE
(Squeeze Me I Cry)

TENOR SAX

Words and Music by HAL HACKADY
and CHARLES NAYLOR

SILVER AND GOLD

Music and Lyrics by
JOHNNY MARKS

SILVER BELLS

from the Paramount Picture THE LEMON DROP KID

Words and Music by JAY LIVINGSTON
and RAY EVANS

Moderately

THAT'S CHRISTMAS TO ME

TENOR SAX

Words and Music by KEVIN OLUSOLA
and SCOTT HOYING

Moderately

SILENT NIGHT

TENOR SAX

Words by JOSEPH MOHR
Translated by JOHN F. YOUNG
Music by FRANZ X. GRUBER

SING WE NOW OF CHRISTMAS

Traditional French Carol

SOMEWHERE IN MY MEMORY

from the Twentieth Century Fox Motion Picture HOME ALONE

TENOR SAX

Words by LESLIE BRICUSSE
Music by JOHN WILLIAMS

Gently and with simplicity

THE STAR CAROL

Lyric by WIHLA HUTSON
Music by ALFRED BURT

Tenderly, with much expression

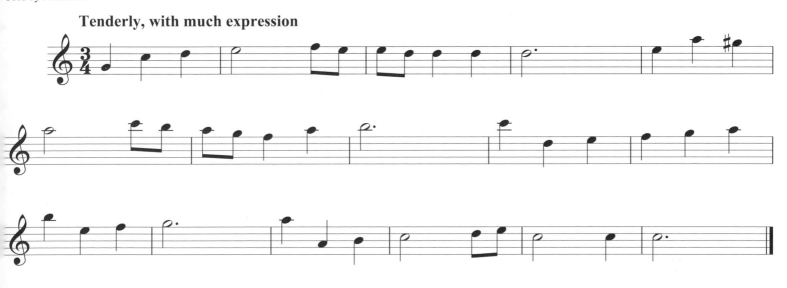

THIS CHRISTMAS

TENOR SAX

Words and Music by DONNY HATHAWAY
and NADINE McKINNOR

TOYLAND
from BABES IN TOYLAND

TENOR SAX

Words by GLEN MacDONOUGH
Music by VICTOR HERBERT

Slowly

UP ON THE HOUSETOP

Words and Music by
B.R. HANBY

Brightly

WE NEED A LITTLE CHRISTMAS

from MAME

TENOR SAX

Music and Lyric by
JERRY HERMAN

THE TWELVE DAYS OF CHRISTMAS

TENOR SAX

Traditional English Carol

*These bars are played a different number of times for each verse.

WE WISH YOU THE MERRIEST

TENOR SAX

Words and Music by
LES BROWN

WE THREE KINGS OF ORIENT ARE

TENOR SAX

Words and Music by
JOHN H. HOPKINS, JR.

Moderately

WE WISH YOU A MERRY CHRISTMAS

Traditional English Folksong

Gaily

WHAT ARE YOU DOING NEW YEAR'S EVE?

TENOR SAX

By FRANK LOESSER

WONDERFUL CHRISTMASTIME

TENOR SAX

Words and Music by
PAUL McCARTNEY

WHAT CHILD IS THIS?

TENOR SAX

Words by WILLIAM C. DIX
16th Century English Melody

Moderately slow

WHITE CHRISTMAS
from the Motion Picture Irving Berlin's HOLIDAY INN

Words and Music by
IRVING BERLIN

Slowly, in 2

YOU'RE ALL I WANT FOR CHRISTMAS

Words and Music by GLEN MOORE
and SEGER ELLIS

Slowly and evenly

THE WONDERFUL WORLD OF CHRISTMAS

TENOR SAX

Words by CHARLES TOBIAS
Music by AL FRISCH